Swear Word Coloring Book 55 Sweary Designs:

Relaxing Adult Swear Words Adult Coloring Book Coloring Book For Fun

Copyright: Published in the United States
By James Spranger
Publisher September 23, 2017

ISBN-13: 978-1977609748

ISBN-10: 1977609740

Asshole

Asshole

Basic
bitch

Bellend

Bitch
Face

Bitchy

Brass
Balls

COLLAB!
BUB B

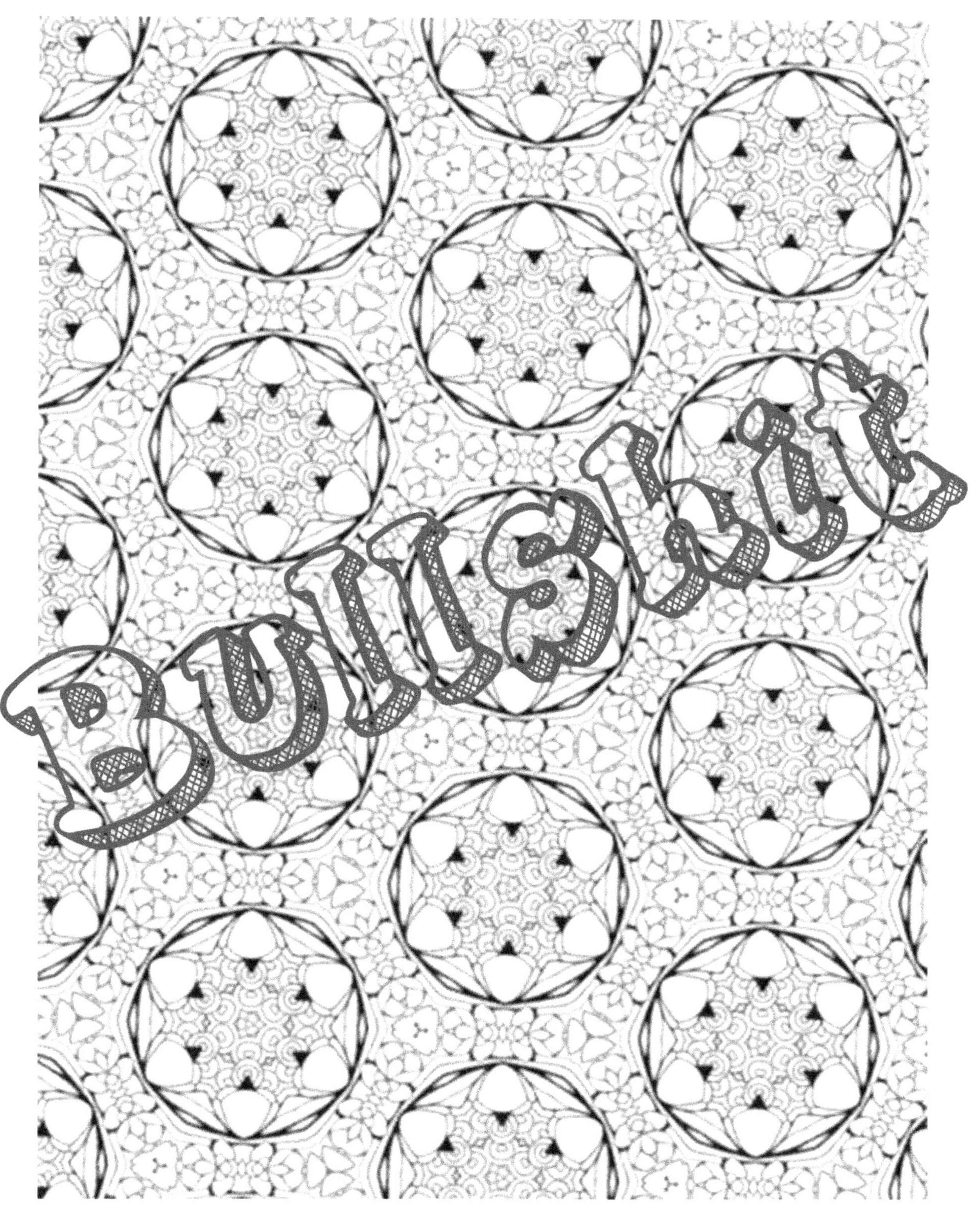
Bullshit

Calm Your Balls

Beautiful

Can't Fix
Stupid

CRAP

Cunt a
saurus
rex

Cuntface

CUNT
FACE

Dickhead
©RicLDP

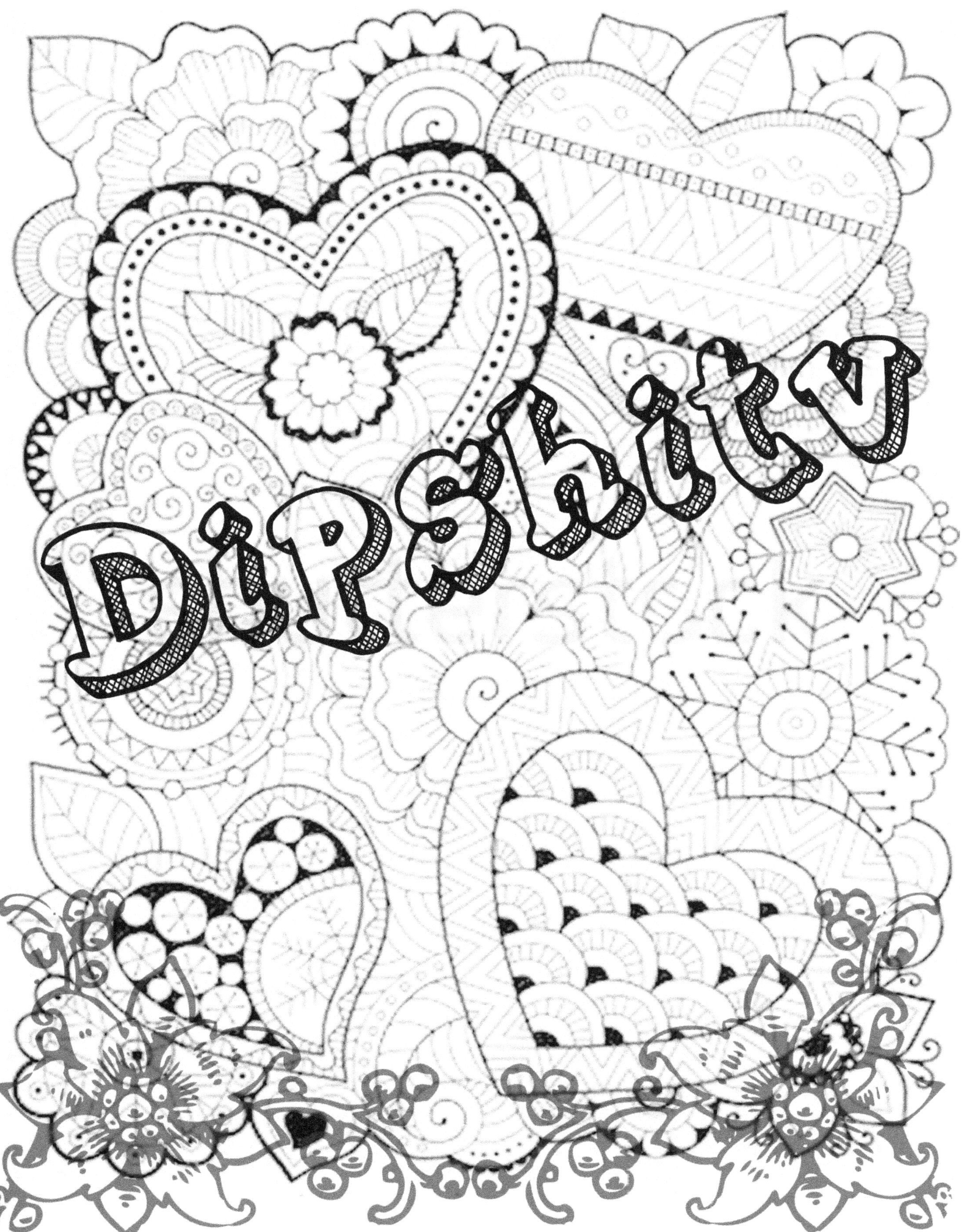
Dipshitv

DOUCHE
BAG

Dumb

DAMN

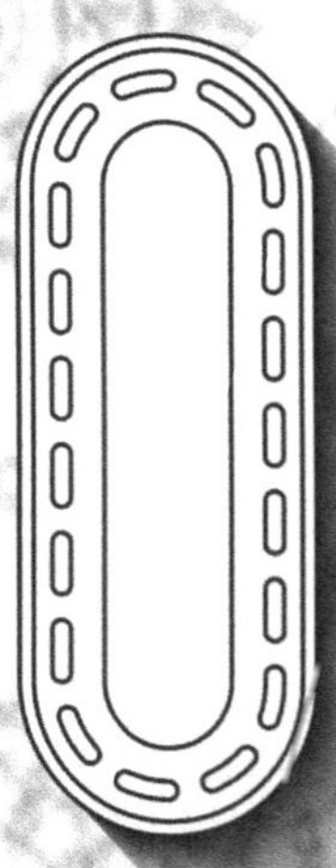

I

T

bite me

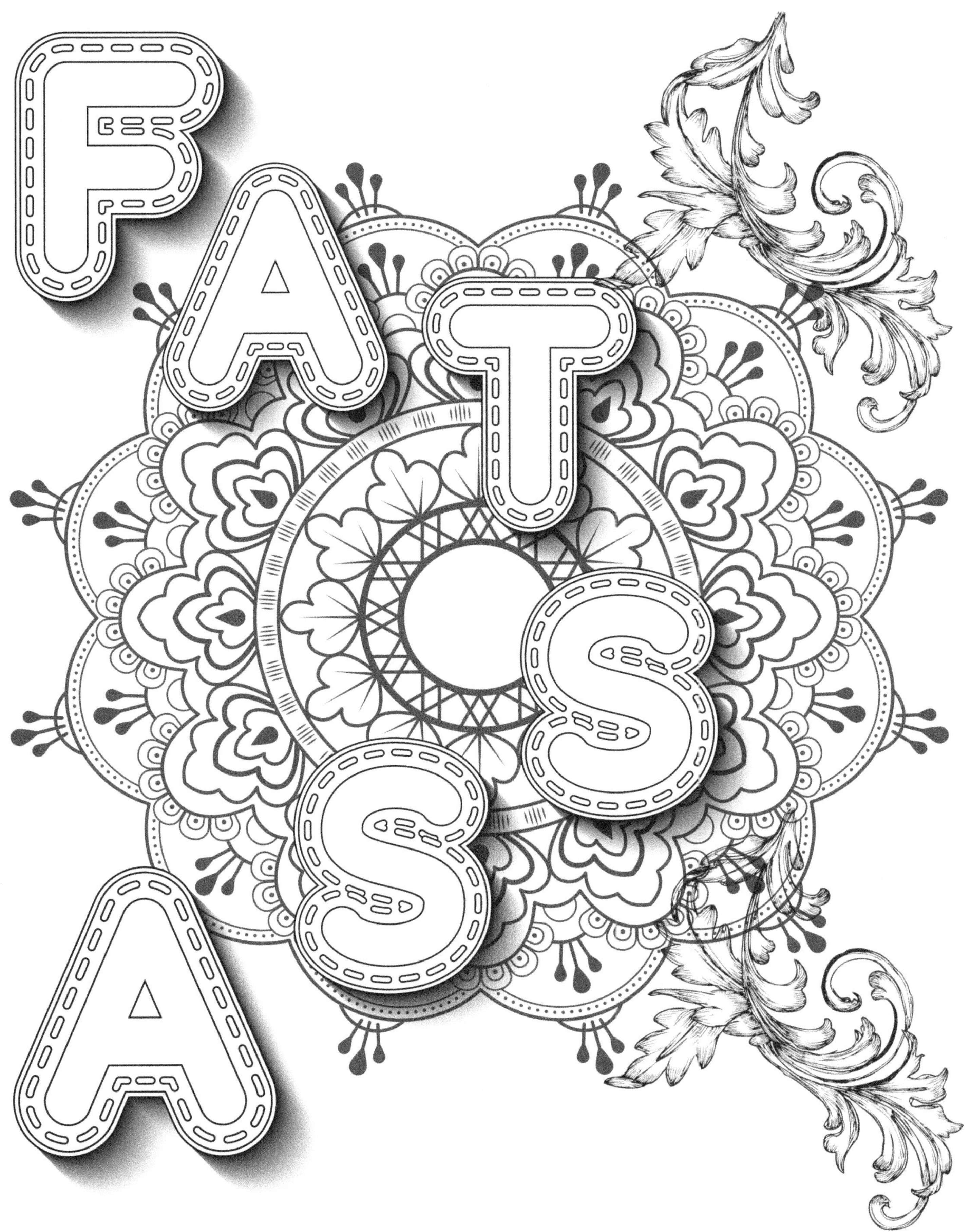

FAT
ASS
A

C
FOR
CHRIST'S
SAKE

FOR
GODNESS

I'M
too hot
TO BE
SAD

FUCK
OFF

FUCK That
Shit

FUCK YOU

Fuck
Your
Self

FuckFace

Fucknut

GO TO
HELL
BITCH

Holy
crap!

Holy Shit

Holy Shit

It's
Freaking
Hot

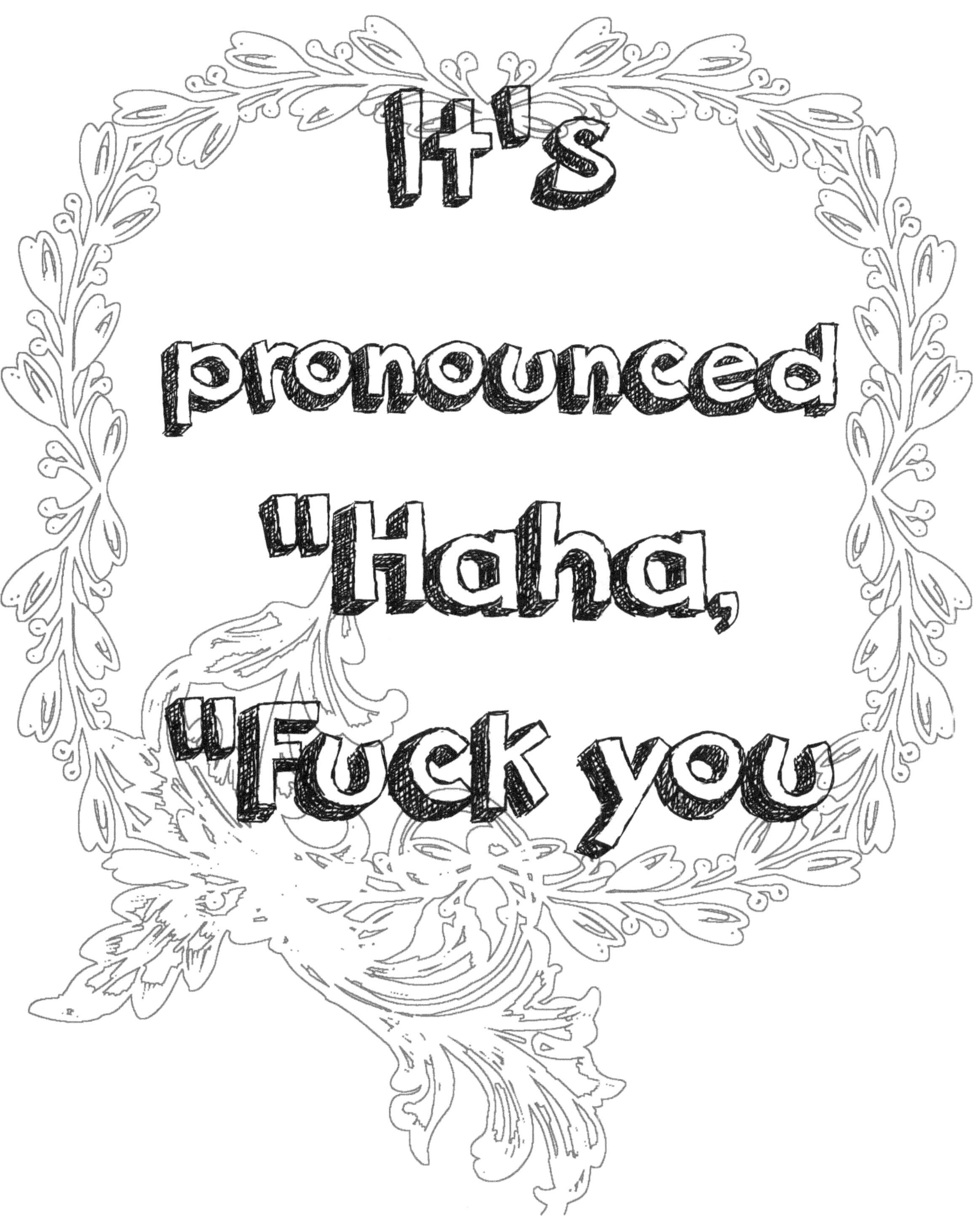

It's
pronounced
"Haha,
"Fuck you

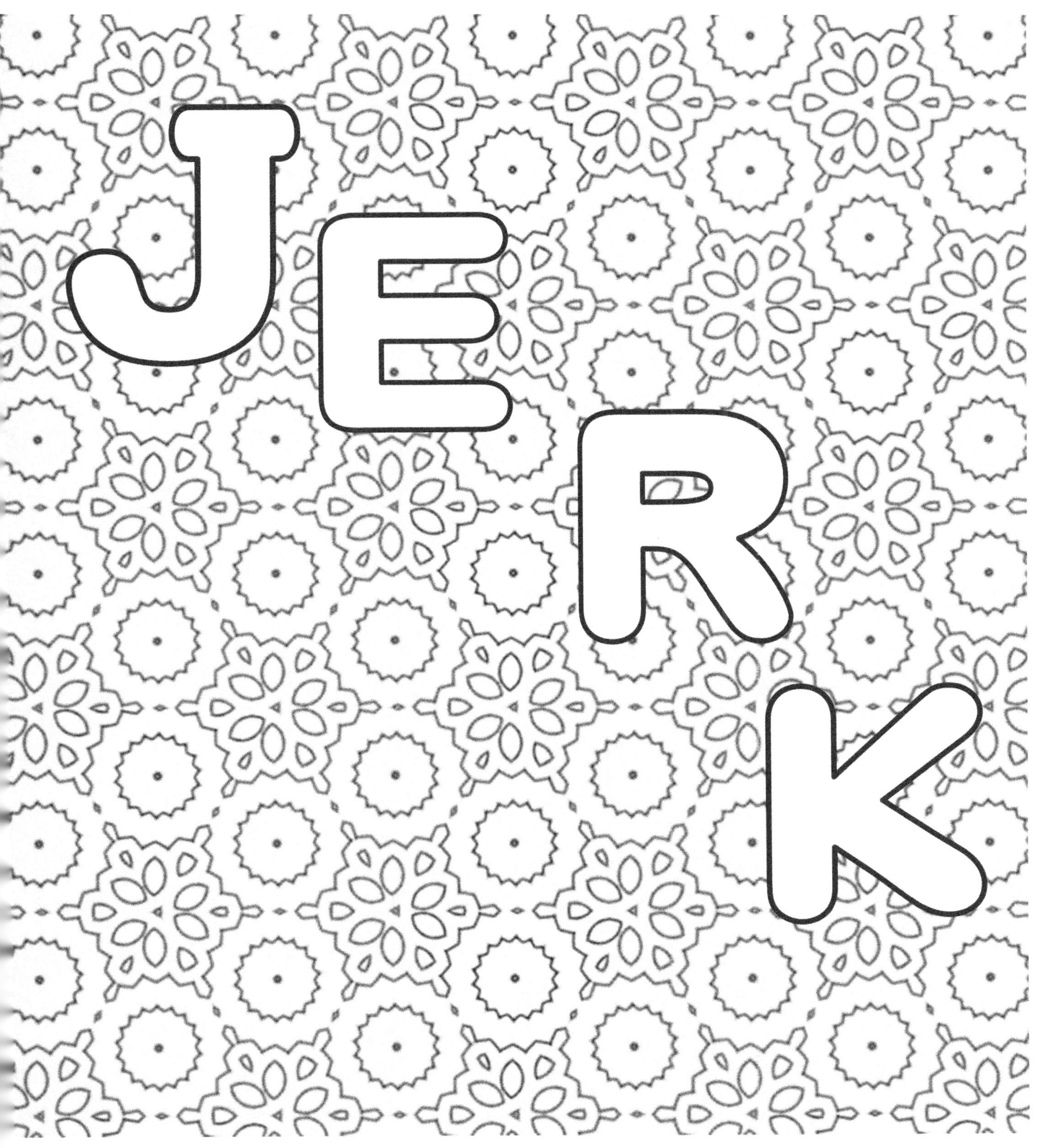

JERK

Lameass

Let
That
Shit Go

OH!
GOD

Oh, Fuck
Cunt

Piece of Shit

PISS
OFF

Pussy

Screw
You

SHIT

Shitbag

SHUT UP

Suck

BATTY

9 781977 609748